Maritza

In the Storm

Pray seek and journal your way to God's Joy

I pray you are encouraged to find God's joy. Remember God will not waste your pain.

IN His joy

Desiree

Desiree Montalvo Holt

In the Storm: **Pray Seek and Journal Your Way to God's Joy**

Copyright© 2019 by Desiree Montalvo-Holt

Anabeka Inc. Publishing
www.anabekainc.com

Book Creation & Design
DHBonner Virtual Solutions, LLC
www.dhbonner.net

Cover Design and Photography
Beatriz Garcia
www.koabluephotography.com

ISBN: 978-0-9885981-6-4

Printed in the United States of America

Contents

Dedicated to *all who are battling a storm...*

"No weapon that is formed against
you shall prosper..."
~ Isaiah 54:17

Acknowledgments

To my husband… God so knew I would need you at such a time as this. I love you. Thank you for sharing your heart with me.

To my beautiful family—especially my son and daughter—without you and your love, Desiree's world would be so empty. The care and love you have poured into me surpasses anything I could have ever dreamed of.

To all of my friends and amazing doctors… your support and encouragement will forever live in my heart. You know exactly who you are.

Finally, to my mom—*my dragonfly*—your love will forever be what drives me. I pray that many will be blessed and experience God's love and true joy!

PRAY

*"Therefore I say to you, whatever things you ask
when you pray, believe that you receive them,
and you will have them."*
~ Mark 11:24

Take five to ten minutes to connect with God. Reflect on your
life and have daily conversations with God. Remember prayer is
a two-way conversation where you not only share your heart but
listen to what He has to say to you as well.

SEEK

*"Seek the Lord and His strength,
seek his face continually."*
~ 1 Chronicles 16:11

Listen to His still voice as you read through the prayers. Come to
Him with a desire to know Him and understand His purpose for
your story.

JOURNAL

*"...write the vision and make it plain on tablets,
that He may run who reads it."*
~ Habakkuk 2:2

Write it down and give your storms fully to the Lord. The reward
is truly pure joy! There is nothing He cannot handle for you.

Introduction

So *joyful* you are here!

Join me as I tell you about how my "joy" journey began...

As a child, I loved to express myself through writing. Putting pen to paper was something that came easily to me. It allowed me to go somewhere alone with my emotions. Writing and journaling took me out of my dark moments and filled me with hope.

In 1996, my early twenties, the struggles in my marriage had become real. I began to journal as a way of escape. In those pages, I poured out my frustration, my fears, and my failures. My journal became a place where I poured out the emotions that stirred within me. As I wrote about my inner turmoil, all I could do was hope that God was listening.

Around this time, I was diagnosed with Hodgkin's Lymphoma. As I endured months of radiation, I decided to write letters to my young son. I did not believe I would be around for long and I wanted my son to know how much I loved him. I wanted him to get to know me through my journal entries.

Years passed, and I was still here! How awesome is God!

I know now that God kept me here for so much more than I could possibly imagine. When my daughter was born, my journal entries evolved into sharing my thoughts, hopes, and dreams for both of my children. I journaled for God to protect them. With each entry, I found myself connecting more and more to God in those pages and His word. I asked Him why I was facing so many struggles. I expressed my anger many times at my circumstances. Still, I was very grateful for being alive.

Soon, I began to close my entries with a prayer to God. I begged Him to see me in my pain and to give me the strength to move forward.

I was hooked!

Writing in my journals became my haven, my safe place. My journal was the place I met up with God and emptied my heart and soul before Him. In return, with every prayer, He began to pour peace and joy into my heart. Prayers started to be answered.

Some were not answered the way I expected, but surely His perfect plan for me was in motion. I felt as if God had finally read my journals and was there with me through all of the stages of my life. I began not only to close my entries with prayer but started to open His word and seek Him more.

I sensed His presence covering me like a warm blanket on a cold brisk day. Now, I not only closed my entries with prayer, but my greatest joy came from connecting to my Heavenly Father in my journals.

After over twenty years of praying, seeking and journaling, I have found true **JOY** in my battles. Now, while I have been suffering from chronic illness for the last eight years, He has shown me to choose Him over my circumstances and to trust Him in the storms.

I am so grateful that when my days seem impossible with pain, infection, and lack of energy, I have learned to surrender to my King; I have learned to pray, seek and journal believing that in my pain and struggles, my God is intentional and purposeful.

In His presence, I have found an inward peace and contentment regardless of the situation I find myself in. My journal entries and prayers have brought me to this place right here where I can share this devotional with you and the words God has placed in my heart.

I have sought Him and allowed Him to comfort and give me strength. Seeking His Joy has become a daily action that has kept me connected to something so much greater than myself. If I have learned anything, it is that God does not waste pain. He will inspire you to bless others, and His joy will bring you through.

My prayer is that when you read each entry and listen to the prayers He has given me to share with you, you are encouraged to share your story and bless someone else with the joy He has placed in you.

He is My God

"Ah, Lord God! Behold, You have made the heavens and the earth by Your great power and outstretched arm. Nothing is too hard for You."

~ Jeremiah 32:17

met God again in my room on the 5th floor of the hospital. He was there. He never left me through the storm. I just had to open my eyes long enough to see Him and long enough to feel His love and purpose for my life.

I met Him head-on, devastated when all my surgeries had failed. *Lord, why?* I did not understand. I was numb for a few days, and silence crept in. My thoughts started to take over, "Lord, I have done all You have asked of me," I cried out. "Why can't I move on without carrying this burden with me?"

He stood there watching as He allowed this trial to unravel, hurting and suffering for me. Like a parent watching His child fall off a bike for the very first time, wanting to pick them up but allowing the fall for them to learn.

Yes, I was desperate at that point, and I needed God to work out a miracle. I wanted a miracle, and I wanted the healer to take all of it away. I did not need another lesson, this I thought. All I can hear as He met me in that dark place was, "Do you trust me, Desiree?" All I could cry out was, "I do, I do!" but I still didn't understand the "why."

What I learned after many days, was that the "why" did not matter. My focus had to shift from the fact that things did not turn out as I thought or planned. I had to trust and believe in His plan in my circumstances. He showed up and reminded me to trust Him regardless of the circumstances. On that bed, He reminded me, He was in control and would pull me through it. All I had to do was trust. This has not been an easy task, but every time I am falling, my trust meter has risen. His plan has been so intentional and purposeful.

What I do get today, is that if I hold on to the emotions of my flesh, I will fall apart, but every time I choose Him through the hard moments I continue to feel such peace and joy, and I know His work in me is for a great purpose.

Will you trust Him with your circumstances?

PRAY

Lord, today I choose to trust You. I want to learn to let go of the pain one day at a time and take hold of Your promises and joy every day.

2

Help me to trust You through the circumstances and not dwell on the situation I am in. Help me to seek You through the pain and struggle even when anger, disappointment, and despair creep into my soul. Guide me in getting to know You better so that my life mirrors all of You in me.

Holy Spirit, teach me how to live in what I can do, not in what I can't do. Keep me focused on the positive so I won't collapse in my flesh and my desires. Give me peace in my story and help me to accept it is different because Your plan for my life is different.

Heal me from the inside out. So, I can enjoy You Lord in my heart and see Your work in me. Be the author. I want to trust You with what You are doing in my life. Teach me how to enjoy the good days and trust You with those moments I just don't understand.

I want to learn to be grateful, Lord, and to be completely transformed and renewed by Your love for me.

Lord, today I choose to trust You in my circumstances.

SEEK AND JOURNAL

Write down your struggles. In each struggle, He will show you the impossible is possible with Him.

"...Jesus looked at them and said to them, "With men this is impossible, but with God all things are possible." ~ Matthew 19:26

"For with God nothing will be impossible. ~ Luke 1:37

"Lift up your eyes and look to the heavens: Who created all these? He who brings out the starry hosts one by one and calls forth each of them by name. Because of His great power and mighty strength, not one of them is missing." ~ Isaiah 40:26 (NIV)

He is My Trust

**"Trust in the Lord with all your heart,
and lean not on your own understanding;"**
~ Proverbs 3:5

D o you believe that by His stripes you are healed, not just physically but emotionally and spiritually? When you are in the storm, do you see God fighting for you or against you? I don't know about you, but I have to share where I am today in hopes that it helps someone in their storm.

Today, I trust He is so much more for me than He ever has been before. Why? My struggles have allowed me to experience Him like no other time in my life. I have had to fall before Him and fully trust in His purpose and plan for my life.

You see, before this battle, I use to say things like, "If this happens to me, or if that happens to me Lord, just take me, please!" Now that He has taken me through it and I have been in it, the experience has given me a strength that I know is just from Him.

I am so grateful!

How this all happened, I am not sure. What I am sure of is that He continues to mold me through it all and I feel like a conqueror with Him. I know He is for me and surely not against me. I don't have to give up; He has a plan. I might not be able to see it, but He loves me and will pull me through it.

I am His child, made in His image and He desires full healing for me. I understand now that what He has planned for me might lead me down some rough roads, but the struggles will create the amazing person He envisioned all along.

Will you yield to Him and trust His purpose for whatever you are going through today?

PRAY

Holy Spirit, I yield to You today. I stand before You, believing that my trials will be purposeful and for Your glory! When my thoughts want to take over, and I am consumed by the moments, remind me, Father, that You are working miracles through me. I am Your amazing design, and You will not leave my side or waste my pains.

Lord, when my body, my mind or my spirit is under attack, teach me how to run to You and Your word. To rest in Your strength and not my own.

I am so grateful that You are aware of everything that is happening to me right now, and You have promised not to leave me. I stand firm in Your plans and know that all the things you allow are intentional.

Help me to be spiritually minded today and to get closer and closer to You in prayer. I release all of my anxieties to You today and trust in Your will for my life.

Lord, I want to be free of me today and wholly filled with You. I want to live in an ongoing conversation with You, believing all You have for me is a blessing to show Your amazing love to others.

Help me to live out Your plan for my life and refuse to give up. I want to find Your peace in all of my messy moments.

SEEK AND JOURNAL

Trust Him with everything today. Share your victories in conversation with Him.

"Those who know Your name will put their trust in You, for you; For You Lord, have not forsaken those who seek You." ~ Psalm 9:10

"But as for me, I trust in You, O Lord; I say, "You are my God." ~ Psalm 31:14

"Now may the God of hope fill you with all joy and peace in believing, that you may abound in hope by the power of the Holy Spirit." ~ Romans 15:13

He is My Father

"Call to Me, and I will answer you,
and show you great and mighty things,
which you do not know."
~ Jeremiah 33:3

Where do you go to find a place to connect with Your Father?

Usually, I sit on my balcony with coffee in hand, some good worship music, my journals, and my Bible. When that doesn't work, I go into my closet where I have post-its with verses that I have needed when praying for my marriage, my children and my health.

If all that fails, I fall on my knees praying for God to help me, with the dumb things that come out of my mouth or the emotions that have me flying off the handle with my spouse or with my kids.

Can you relate?

In these chaotic prayer moments, I am so grateful to have this time to find my Father, the one who listens and who does not chastise me for my silly mishaps. I am so grateful for His love and His constant open-door policy. I am thankful for where He has me at this time, totally trusting Him in all things.

I may still say the wrong things or do the wrong things, I am human, after all, but I know I am no longer just seeing Him in the distance. In my wrong moments, I am now learning to walk with Him hand in hand. I am learning to truly trust that even in my fears, He is there. My life and my thoughts are so different now with Him.

I am so grateful for the journey, as I go, once again, into a surgery room. I know that, though my flesh is not at ease, my spirit is, because He has held me through this test. He has taught me through this test. He has been so intentional. Relying on my Father and trusting His will has transformed my life.

Will you sit with your Father today and experience life with Him?

PRAY

Father, I invite You in to fill the pages of this story. Continue to increase my faith with Your love. Through the trials, help me to seek and find Your Joy, to believe that my story is an ongoing manifestation of Your amazing love for my life.

Today, I choose to sit in my quiet place with You and listen to Your words. I choose to be consumed by the wisdom that only You can give me.

I yearn for Your instructions in my times of fear and unbelief. Show me Your will for my life, Lord. I am ready!

I welcome Your Holy Spirit inside all of my anxious moments. Calm me and show me Your plans. Fill me, Lord, and create in me a person that sees You in all of the activities of the day.

Lord, I sit and trust You over my body, over my heart, over every part of my being. I am Your magnificent creation, Your ongoing masterpiece. Allow me to walk with You and to know You more intimately each day.

What a great feeling to know that in my emptiness, You are the only one who can make me full again.

Overwhelm me with Your strength as I face the challenges of the day. Armor me with a faith that can push through and conquer all of the obstacles of the day.

Still me, today, with Your word. Lead me to that quiet place where I can only hear Your voice. Today, I want to rest in Your arms so that I can find peace in your presence, Father.

SEEK AND JOURNAL

Find a quiet place and seek Your Father in these verses.

So, my dear friends, listen carefully; those who embrace these my ways are most blessed. Mark a life of discipline and live wisely; don't squander your precious life. Blessed the man, blessed the woman, who listens to me, awake and ready for me each morning, alert and responsive as I start my days' work."
~ Proverbs 8:32-35 (MSG)

"Seek the Lord and His strength; Seek His face evermore!"
~ I Chronicles 16:11

He is My Guide

"These things I have spoken to you, that in Me you may have peace. In the world you will have tribulation; but be of good cheer, I have overcome the world."

~ John 16:33

Every morning, my goal is to spend time with the Lord. I go out on my balcony with a cup of coffee and His word. In these moments I sit and wonder how my life would be if I had chosen my way and not His way. I ask God, "Why did You let me go this way? Or say, "Wow! You really were there during the storm."

I am always in awe when I look back, and He shows me how He was there, even when I choose to reject His path.

During this time, I am so humbled by His love for me and how He has met my every need and saved my every tear. Don't let me fool you; I cannot clearly see this during the storm. But, when my head gets out of that muddy place, I see His amazing grace and cannot imagine life without Him.

I know some needs He does not meet because there was a lesson there for me to learn. Trust me; I have learned this the hard way. I genuinely understand after many years of falling and getting angry, that He knows best. Of course, I could not see this at the moment.

How about you?

Just like a child is to her parent, I know now He is my Father, my Provider! I am so glad that my trials and wrong turns have kept me desperate for Him and have led me into His will today. I am not perfect, but I know He is.

Will you join me today in giving Him praise for the trials in our lives that provide us with wisdom and draw us closer to Him.

PRAY

Lord, thank you for being my ultimate provider. Thank you for never giving up on me even when I have been ready to give up on myself and those around me. Thank you for never leaving my side, even when I pushed You away, You stood, watched, and shed tears for me, but You never left me.

Lord, even when I did not know the consequences of the road I was traveling, You guided and taught me through it, You lifted me up when I had no more energy to give in my flesh, and You reminded me You were there.

No matter how many times I have failed You, You always let me know You love me and will never give up on me. My heart is saddened knowing that I have hurt You in my decisions as Your child. I am sorry.

I want You to know, Father, that I am so thankful that each morning is brand new with You, another chance to get it right with You. I am so grateful that Your word has such great promises:

> *Be strong and of good courage, do not fear nor be afraid of them, for the LORD your God, He is the One who goes with you. He will not leave you nor forsake you."* ~ Deuteronomy 31:6

When life seems to fail me, Father, You don't. Lord, help me to seek You through the lonely roads, through the wrong turns, through the difficult trials that I do not comprehend. Help me to live in your will and purpose.

Lord, today I choose to glorify your name. I choose Your love and embrace. I choose the promises in Your word that give me life and hope for every victory and battle I go through each day.

Lord, I exchange my trails and bumpy roads for Your peace. Take my hand and lead me.

When the tough times come, remind me you are MY FATHER and will never leave me. When I want to run, push me closer to You.

Move me to praise and worship You through it all. Teach me how to rejoice when I cannot see what You have in store for me.

Immerse me, Father, in Your embrace.

SEEK AND JOURNAL

Write down the trials you are going through. Give them to your Father and thank Him for all the trials He has fought—and is fighting—for you.

He is My Dwelling Place

> *"He who dwells in the secret place of the Most High shall abide under the shadow of the Almighty. I will say of the Lord, "He is my refuge and my fortress; my God, in Him I will trust."*
> ~ Psalm 91:1-2

A re you finding peace in your dwelling place? What is that place for you? If you are like me, you dwell in all the wrong places: in other people's Facebook pages, Instagram posts, Tweets and feel like, wow, I am pretty boring!

Is that only me?

Often, all I find is uncertainty and chaos, especially in the events of our world. If I dwell long enough on others, TV or social media, my anxiety about the future quickly consumes me.

Do you know that you do not have to depend on or dwell in these places and feel depleted? We have the choice every day, every morning to dwell in our King's home and drink from our Lord's living water! The choice to step away and live with peace knowing He has allowed certain things for our good and His Divine purpose. Your life won't be trouble-free, but believe me, the struggles will be easier to go through daily if you remain close to Him.

Today, are you ready to turn off the noises that disrupt your peace and dwell with Him so that you do not grow weary?

PRAY

Father, I want to draw closer and closer to You each moment of my day. When I am drawn to the events of my daily life and the world around me wants to take over my thoughts, my ways, and my life, teach me how to remain fully in Your presence.

I am not worthy of the grace You offer me each day, especially when I continuously draw away from You and then run right back to You in my day. I am so thankful that You are such a loving and caring Father. I thank You today for the constant opportunity to choose You willingly and freely.

Holy Spirit, I yearn to be in Your presence. Shower me with Your love and wash me clean of all the nonsense polluting my mind and disrupting my peace. Show me how to draw from Your living water of knowledge and armor me with Your strength. Gear me, today for battle, to defeat all that comes my way.

Forgive me, Father, when in my weakness I allow my flesh to take over and I fail to choose Your way. Renew my spirit so that I can follow only Your path. I no longer want to just visit with You; now, I hunger to remain fully with You. Ignite my faith, Lord. Fill my heart so that I can rejoice in Your grace and mercies.

Today, I choose to dwell with You, my Creator, in Your place. Thank you for extending Your grace and love to me over and over again.

SEEK AND JOURNAL

Dwell in His wisdom. Seek and know that He is God. Write down what you hear from Him and seek His wisdom in the following verses.

"Be my rock of refuge, to which I can always go; give the command to save me, for you are my rock and my fortress." ~ Psalm 71-3 (NIV)

"One thing I have desired of the Lord, that will I seek: that I may dwell in the house of the Lord all the days of my life, to behold the beauty of the Lord, and to inquire in His temple." ~ Psalm 27:4-5

"Because you have made the Lord, who is my refuge, even the Most High, your dwelling place." ~ Psalm 91:9

He is My Joy

"But without faith, it is impossible to please Him, for he who comes to God must believe that He is, and that He is a rewarder of those who diligently seek him."

~ Hebrews 11:6

So, what is it with me and this Joy thing? Well, let me share a little bit of how I got to this place, a place I would not give up for anything in this world. My journey has been long, and the trials have been tough, but God has been in the center of each one.

I have believed in His purpose, and He has answered. I have trusted—and by His grace—I am still here. Today, I am so Joyful that the walls have come down as I have chosen to lean closer and closer to Him.

You see, God has been there when I sought Him, during the months of radiation, after being diagnosed with Hodgkin's Lymphoma. When the chronic illness wanted to steal my Joy, God showed me how to pray through the hard, miserable moments. He extended His hand, and I grabbed on for dear life. I drew from Him what I did not have inside myself. He reminded me of my beautiful mom, family, and children; the fight was going to be worth it! He allowed this journey and all I had to keep doing was believing, seeking and knowing He was and is always in control, no matter how tough the journey is.

When divorce stepped in, and I felt like I had failed, and the devil wanted to fill my mind with lies, I chose to believe in my King. I chose to seek Him. He filled me with His living water as I drew from Him, and I found Joy in the struggle! He has blessed me over and over again through the storm, and as I learned to pray harder, I asked and sought Him deeper and watched Him work through the losses with me.

When my mother suffered through cancer and joined our King at such an early age, He showed me His Joy through her smile; as she was joining Him in His kingdom. Oh! How the Joy and peace filled my heart then and does today when I think of her. What JOY, my dragonfly!

As I have been living with pain from a condition called, "Fistulas" for over eight years, I still can't believe how my heart rejoices with Joy after multiple surgeries believing and trusting more and more in my King.

Today, believe it or not, I am the most Joyful! I am so grateful that the journey and walk through the dark places have drawn me into His beautiful light. I don't know how it all happened, but I pray that you find this Joy with Him in whatever you are going through.

Don't give up no matter the trial you are in, remember, God is intentional and has a plan. Continue to pray and believe in Him.

Trials won't be easy and won't go away but how amazing is His love that He will carry them with us and through us.

All you have to do is trust in His love; the Joy you will experience will become contagious.

PRAY

Father, how I yearn for You each and every day. How wonderful it is to walk in my trials with You. Lord, everything the devil has intended for bad in my life, You have taken and turned into pure Joy! I am believing, trusting and knowing You will see me through it all.

Teach me how to keep running to Your living water, so that my heart and body never grow weary. Help me, Father, to be thankful for what You have brought me through. Draw me closer and closer to You, dear Lord. May Your love be where I dwell when I am feeling hopeless and defeated. I desire for You to fill each moment of my day with Your presence. Radiate in me, Father, as I take each step forward with You. Help me to take each step holding onto Your hand. Don't let go!

Lift me, Father, when I fall and hold me when my heart is troubled. I can't do this, Lord, without You. I welcome You to my day as My Jehovah Jireh (My provider), My El Olam (Everlasting God) and My El Shaddai (Lord God Almighty). I seek Your will and purpose for my life. As circumstances in my life seem out of place and life seems like too much to bear, still me so I can see Your perfect, unchanging ways and will for my life. I welcome Your Joy, Your way into my life!

SEEK AND JOURNAL

Spend time in His word and believe, seek and know that He is God.

"The Lord looks down from heaven upon the children of men, to see if there are any who understand, who seek God." ~ Psalm 14:2

"But from there you will seek the Lord your God, and you will find Him if you seek Him with all your heart and with all your soul."~ Deuteronomy 4:29

"But seek first the kingdom of God and His righteousness, and all these things shall be added to you." ~ Matthew 6:33

_____

_____

_____

_____

_____

_____

_____

_____

He is My Spirit

"Blessed is she who believed,
for there will be a fulfillment of those things
which were told her from the Lord."
~ Luke 1:45

Where does your Joy come from? Do you believe Joy is God's desire for you each and every day? Do you trust that God's Joy is sufficient to fill your spirit?

If you do, join me in not allowing anything to steal your Joy.

Together in prayer, let's seek God's Joy every morning, even when the days seem impossible. Let us start our day holding and believing that ALL of His promises have been designed by our heavenly Father for our JOY in Him.

Today believe in the….

- Promise that He created you and me to be healthy (Jeremiah 30:17)
- Promise that He created you and me to be prosperous (Matthew 6:31-33)

- Promise that He created you and me to be Joyful when we dwell in His presence (Mark 11:24)

Will you join me in seeking and believing in His JOY?

PRAY

Father, today I choose Joy, Your Joy! I choose to find joy in the wonders of Your creation. I choose to seek Joy when the path in front of me becomes complicated and impossible.

Today, Lord, fill my heart with Your incredible Joy, so there is no room for sadness. I choose today to believe that You created me to be someone extraordinary, designed in Your image with great purpose. Remind me and teach me to no longer ask for what You have already promised but to seek and believe it is already mine!

Help me to live a life fully immersed in Your presence so that the nonsense I create in my mind and flesh falls, only embracing Your peace. Help me to stay focused on the day ahead and to leave the past where it belongs.

Lord, when I fall into those bad habits you have not designed me for, teach me to surrender to Your spirit. Rid me of the lies the devil wants me to believe about myself.

I am believing today that You, through me, can accomplish miracles through my testimonies. I lay before You in prayer and worship so that Joy begins to fill every ounce of my body, and I become the light that shines on others and daily demonstrates You.

SEEK AND JOURNAL

Make a list of those things that bring you Joy. I have added a few extra pages at the end of the devotional for you to list all of the things you are grateful for as you journal. Trust me. This will bring you joy.

_____

_____

_____

_____

_____

_____

_____

_____

_____

_____

_____

_____

Desiree Montalvo-Holt

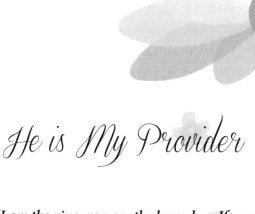

He is My Provider

"I am the vine; you are the branches. If you
remain in me and I in you, you will bear much
fruit; apart from me you can do nothing."
~ John 15:5

Are you hungry? No, not for the food that fills your body, but the nourishment that fills your soul. Do you find yourself getting filled with the messages in magazines, Facebook, Instagram, twitter? How full are you from these sources?

As I sit here contemplating where I find the nourishment to feed my soul, I am reminded of how empty I am at the end of the day when I don't go to the source, "Jesus, our true source of life." I am also reminded of where I have been and where He has brought me from, and I know for sure that if it were not for His grace and mercy, I would not be where I am today, physically, emotionally and spiritually.

Did you know that you are the branch and He is the vine? This is where your real Joy comes from! Living and seeking His joy and peace depends on us drawing from Him daily for life to make sense. I know it does for me. How about you?

When I find myself not drawing from Him, I am limited, lacking fulfillment as He has intended for me to have. I find myself withering away in the turmoil of this world and being drawn away from the One who gives life and promises eternal life.

I know now that to keep going, pushing and believing, I must nourish myself with His word and must keep praying and believing in Him alone. When I look back at all of the times I could have fallen into the devil's traps and drowned and withered away, I am so grateful that He has given us Himself to draw true life from.

Will you draw from the vine and pray for God to be your provider?

PRAY

Today, Father, I fall at Your feet immensely grateful for bringing me to this place of fullness and Joy with You. Help me to seek Your word today and dwell on all of the promises You have for me.

Lord, I know now that when I withdraw myself from Your vine, I grow weary and allow the devil a way in, where You have specifically designed space for Your peace and Joy to dwell.

I want to continue to be fed by You. I desire for You to be the nourishment that satisfies my soul. Lord, today I want to wrap myself around everything You have for me. Prune my branches and cleanse me, Lord, of all the things I need to remove to get closer and closer to You.

Today, I want to draw from You so that I can survive in the midst of all of the storms that come my way. Remind me, heavenly Father, that apart from You I can't do anything.

Teach me how to hit reset with You so that I can do the work You have designed for me to do.

Help me to seek You, know You, and believe fully in You so that others can be blessed with this Joy You have taught me to receive through Your word.

Father, the world cannot fill those voids that life circumstances have created, but Your love and Joy can produce the fruit that You so carefully designed to tell my story.

Lord, today I want to produce Your fruit and stay forever drawing from Your vine. Help me, Father, to stay close to You.

SEEK AND JOURNAL

Spend time in His word and allow God to be the vine you draw Joy and peace from daily.

"You did not choose Me, but I chose you and appointed you that you should go and bear fruit, and that your fruit should remain, that whatever you ask the Father in My name He may give you." ~ John 15:16

"But the fruit of the Spirit is love, joy, peace, longsuffering, kindness, goodness, faithfulness," ~ Galatians 5:22

"Is anyone among you in trouble? Let him pray. Is anyone happy? Let them sing songs of praise." ~ James 5:13 (NIV)

He is My Solace

*"But those who hope in the Lord will renew their strength.
They will soar on wings like eagles; they will run and
not grow weary, they will walk and not be faint."*
~ Isaiah 40:31 (NIV)

There is something about being in an airplane that makes me feel free and totally safe in God's arms. Can't run anywhere or even call anyone. He is watching me on this journey and smiling because He has empowered me to not give up.

He has allowed me to grow through this painful journey and, though at times I pray for Him to take it away, I know His will is perfect for me. Just as I trust a pilot to land us safely, I have to trust in God's perfect will no matter what doctors say.

I can't lose hope, and I have to use what I have learned in the storms to bless someone else and glorify His name.

How will you use your journey, your growing pains?

PRAY

Father, help me to see You in my journey. A journey that was specifically designed by You for my good and to bring me closer to You. The deeper I go into its path, the more I get to know You and understand why You have allowed my trials (Ecclesiastes 3:1).

I am so fragile, Father, without You. Strengthen me in my weaknesses and hold me when my flesh is in fear. Comfort me with Your word and shower me with Your grace.

Abba Father, I thank you for choosing me for such a time like this. (Lamentations 3:25-26) Please help me when I want to give up on everything (Proverbs 3:5-6). I desire to find You every step of the way in the ups and downs of it all.

Teach me how to hold on to hope and immerse myself in Your amazing word so that I can grow and be ready for Your kingdom.

SEEK AND JOURNAL

This week fully trust in His journey for you. Write down all that God shares with you in this time with Him.

Desiree Montalvo-Holt

He is My Heart

"But let all those rejoice who put their trust in You;
let them ever shout for joy, because you defend; let
those also who love Your name be joyful in You."

~ Psalm 5:11

As I sit silently seeking and desiring to hear and connect with God, yearning daily for answers to my health, I constantly hear Him whispering in my ear, "Will you trust me with this one again and again?"

In these moments, He reminds me of my constant desire to want to be in control, and how quickly I forget He is in control.

As I continue to walk in my health issues with many unknowns, my experiences have taught me to walk fervently with Him and continue to trust Him. I want my heart to be open to His will, not my confusion. I am learning to choose JOY over the chaos and surrender to His total will for my life.

PRAY

Father, in my quiet moments, I want to hear You. I want to totally be in Your presence and feel You pour Your love into me.

Guide me today into Your purpose. Don't allow me to lose my trust in You and become impatient in my circumstances. Teach me how to draw from Your power and strength (Psalm 84 5-7). Empower me to represent You even in the storms (2 Chronicles 16:9). As the storms blind me, open up my eyes and clear the path so that I can continue to walk hand in hand with You, even in my circumstances.

Lord, I want to not only trust You in my struggle, but I also want to fall into Your arms and release control to the only one who can! (Psalm 5:11) I want to be in a place of openness with You, Father, where You dwell in my heart, and I consistently choose joy over my confusion.

I am choosing You in my heart today over everything else.

SEEK AND JOURNAL

Allow God to walk with you in your struggle. Release your struggles to Him. What is God asking you to let go off?

_____

_____

_____

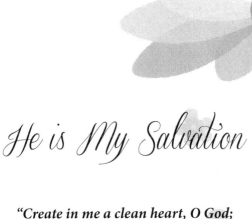

He is My Salvation

"Create in me a clean heart, O God;
and renew a steadfast spirit within me."
~ Psalm 51:10

At times, I try to imagine what God's love for me looks like, the thought of it overwhelms and floods my soul; He loves me no matter how many times I fail Him, no matter how many times I stumble. Over time, in my trials, I see His hands extended, waiting for me to be restored with His love.

I know deep in my heart when I choose His hand and allow Him to carry my burdens, He will help me, and the pain will be easier to bear. So why, Lord, do I keep falling into the same trap?

Do you ever ask yourself this question when you try to carry all of your burdens on your own?

Today, I am determined not to give up. I choose to meet Him each time, knowing He is my rock and my salvation.

Join me in offering your struggles, your burdens to Him and accepting His love and guidance in your Heart.

PRAY

Lord, take my heart today. I close the door to the turmoil and open the door to Your loving spirit. I choose to let You in, so You can cover the scars and bruises on my heart with Your Joy, love, and peace. I no longer want to feel depleted at the end of my days. I want to rejoice in knowing You. Will You, Father, enter my heart and allow me to dwell in Your renewing and restoration of me?

I run to You and place my burdens and struggles at Your feet. Help me carry them, so I can be free to worship and know You better today. I yearn to hand them to You once and for all.

I want to live today in the goodness of Your promises for my life. Mold in me a heart complete with Your love. Embrace me in my trials and shower me with Your grace. Pour Your love into my heart like clean running water, so that I can pour love to those around me as You would want me to do.

Change me, God; mold me into the image of You!

Help me today to adhere to Your ways, so that I can free myself of the vicious cycles that want to steal my Joy each and every day. I want my heart to be free and rejoice in the love that You offer me freely each day.

I let you in, Father; into every part of me. Please change me, change my actions and let them be a reflection of You.

I need You to dwell and be in my Heart today, Lord.

SEEK AND JOURNAL

Spend time in His word and let Him begin to renew your Heart and carry your burdens.

"Be anxious for nothing, but in everything by prayer and supplication, with thanksgiving, let your requests be made known to God;" ~ Phil. 4:6-7

"My flesh and my heart may fail; but God is the strength of my heart and my portion forever." ~ Psalm 73:26

"Trust in the Lord with all your heart, and lean not on your own understanding; in all your ways acknowledge Him, and He shall direct your paths." ~ Proverbs 3:5-6

He is My Comforter

*"Let all those who seek You rejoice and be glad
in You; and let those who love Your salvation
say continually, Let God be magnified!"*
~ Psalm 70:4

Have you ever been in a situation where your anxiety level was off the roof? Well, today's prayer came to me on a plane ride with my husband that was undoubtedly one of those days.

We had visited doctors, and the news was not good—more surgeries, more traveling and more time off work and living in hotels. My hubby, who is usually even-keeled in these situations, was a bit aggravated at our flight situation and concerned about the pain I was in.

So, here we were on an overbooked and crowded flight, seated at the very back of the plane, and God saw us and left an empty seat on our row because He knew the trial that we had been through.

Though my medical battles were not ending, God showed us to rejoice for the open seat that allowed us space to move on a five-hour flight. You see, He knew what we needed and needed me to see Him in the small victories. He reminded us He was there through this storm.

Who would have thought that an open seat would cause so much JOY!

PRAY

Lord, today I choose Your Joy. I choose to focus on the small victories, the victories that remind me that You are right there with me all of the time. When my body can move, I choose to rejoice. When my legs can walk, and arms can move, I rejoice... knowing you alone allow it.

Father, I cannot see the final masterpiece or imagine the magnificence of Your final product in me, but today I choose to rejoice knowing You got me! Every little piece of me belongs to You alone. You consistently remind me when I want to take control of each moment; You alone are the Abba Father. You are the beginning and the end.

You know the exact place where I belong; You are in control of me.

All You ask of me is to love, believe and seek You Lord. So, today Lord, I choose You! I choose to rejoice when I can't, and You can.

I choose to rejoice when I fall, and You are there to sustain me. I choose to rejoice when my heart beats, and You allow me another day. I choose to rejoice and learn through the trials, through the pains, and through it all because You chose me for a time like this.

So, I once again choose to move out of Your way and wait patiently on Your timing. I choose to focus on small victories. I choose Joy because You give it to us as a gift. It frees me from carrying the heaviness on my own.

I choose You, MY COMFORTER, and lay it all at Your feet, knowing and believing that only You know the molding and shaping it will take for this finished product to be ready for Your kingdom.

Thank you, Father, for showing up in an open seat.

SEEK AND JOURNAL

Are you ready to Rejoice today? Make a list of all of your small victories. What was your "open seat" moment?

_____

_____

_____

_____

_____

_____

_____

_____

_____

He is My Emotions

"The voice of one crying in the wilderness: "Prepare the way of the Lord; make straight in the desert a highway for our God."
~ Isaiah 40:3

Do you ever get upset and just can't let it go? You need answers, apologies, explanations before you can free yourself from the chains you have allowed to shackle you?

Yep, that would surely be me. I just get in that funk and can't seem to find a way out on my own. I can't sleep, my head begins to feel like I have a boulder sitting on top of it and my day slowly starts to take a nose dive.

I know in my flesh, and in my head, I will never get out. So, I go to the One who knows me before the mess and chains have me all wrapped up. I go to His word and pray, pray, pray for God to help me see Him in the situations. It still might take me days, but I surely do not give up.

In your storm today, find His peace, love, and joy, and choose Him over Your mess.

PRAY

Lord, I need to see things from Your perspective. I desire deep in my heart to be more and more like You and to get out of my head when things are not going as planned.

Stay close to me in the chaos. Teach me how to let it go and let You fill me with forgiveness and peace in the storms. I want to fall into Your hands and be consumed by Your wisdom in these times when my emotions do not get me anywhere. (Proverbs 1:7)

Please take me from the wilderness, where the weeds are consuming me daily, and show me a clear path (Isaiah 40:3-5).

Father, I know You are a good, good Father, look how far You have brought me from my pains (Isaiah 64:8). I want to continue to be restored by You and Your goodness.

Wrap yourself around me and fill my heart with Your love today!

SEEK AND JOURNAL

Create your own prayer. Start with "Lord, thank you for..."

Desiree Montalvo-Holt

He is My Life

"God is our refuge and strength,
a very present help in trouble."
~ Psalm 46:1

Have you ever planned your week to go great and all was going smoothly until something hit you from left field and threw your whole week off? Maybe, it was long hours at work. A sick child, you all of a sudden had to pick up at school. A sick parent you had to tend to, or maybe you caught a bad cold and could not move forward with your to-do list.

I am sure it has happened to most of you because it seems to happen to me quite often. I often look up and say, "Okay, God. I get it." I just need to worry about the now and let You handle the tomorrow, as tomorrow is not guaranteed for any of us." It is during these weeks and days when all has gone in the opposite direction of what I planned I am glad my life is in His hands. He can take all this mess and turn it into His Joy!

He can bring good from what I see as bad and give me peace until the storm calms down.

PRAY

Father, I am so grateful my life entirely belongs to You. I give you my hours, days and weeks. Help me to plan them with You in mind the whole time through. (Luke 12:22-26)

Teach me how to work through the emotions that keep me stressed and draw me into my messy places. Take over. I want to take the time to be fully immersed in Your word so I can hear Your guiding voice.

Your word clearly says we should not plan past today, as tomorrow is not guaranteed. Help me to remember this as I create my to-do list. I give you every area of my life, Holy Spirit. (Jeremiah 29:11)

I want to take every step with You, Father. I rejoice in You and desire to stay close and never lose sight of Your love. (Psalm 94:19)

Thank you once again for choosing me to be Yours.

SEEK AND JOURNAL

Remember not to think too far ahead. God is in full control. Give Him your to-do list.

He is My Story

"Arise, shine; for your light has come!
And the glory of the Lord is risen upon you."
~ Isaiah 60:1

God woke me up today as I was listening to our pastor speak about sharing your story. I tend not to want to dwell on my story, and more on the joy I find, when I give Him my pain and struggles. I am not one who likes to draw attention to the details of my health. Yet, God keeps telling me that my story has a purpose and I must share to help others who need to see what He is doing—*and going to do*—through it.

I am not here to fool you or be anyone's hero. I am none of that! My life is imperfect, messy and truly impossible some days. Days like yesterday, when in the midst of a really bad health day, I had to cry it out, take a deep breath and say, God, "You promised good out of this!" So, with Him as my strength, I picked myself up and went at it again.

Days like these are hard for me and my family. My health has affected many areas of my life. I cannot sit and pretend that it has not. God continues to remind me that He will not waste my pain.

God is watching, even as I dwindle emotionally and physically in my own strength, and although I might not be able to see it at this moment or understand it, His goodness keeps showing up in the darkness, and I pray His purpose and will are accomplished through me.

What is your story? Who can you bless with your story today?

PRAY

Lord, be the author of my story today. Father, let the words and all of its content be for my good and Your glory. Breathe life into my soul and energize my spirit. (Matthew 5:6)

Inspire me through Your word to be open with my story. To share with those who need to see You and Your goodness. Continue to take me to Your place of joy and complete me with Your love.

Holy Spirit, when my flesh is so weak, and I am ready to give up, teach me how to stay immersed in You. (Romans) 8:26

I want to live fully in Your presence so my story and its pages include all You have designed just for me. Teach me how to be the light in someone's life through this amazing journey You have placed me on. (Ephesians 5:7-8)

Thank you for using me and trusting me with this, Your story!

SEEK AND JOURNAL

Write down your story. Pray about who you can bless with it.
God is right there with you, and He loves you so much.

He is My Guide

"And we all, who with unveiled faces contemplate the Lord's glory, are being transformed into His image with ever-increasing glory, which comes for the Lord, who is the Spirit."
~ 2 Corinthians 3:18 (NIV

As my journey continues and the pages to my story fill up quickly, do I allow my pages to be filled with my emotions, or with what the doctors are saying, or do I fully trust in God's will and plan for my life?

As I struggle back and forth with the decision, I know that listening to God and allowing Him to do His work through my circumstances, will fill me with the ultimate Joy that I seek daily.

Today, as I struggle with the many overwhelming areas of my life, I am choosing Him over my chaos. I am staying focused on His plan, not the doctors or what the world says is wrong with me. No matter what the symptoms or medical reports say, God will be there, and today that is all I can believe and stand on! The alternative causes me too much stress.

So, will you trust Him with your story and allow Him to be part of the writing in your pages today?

Father, today, as I seek You in your word, I am so grateful for my story that was uniquely designed by You. Thank you for having favor over my life and for giving me the freedom from carrying these problems on my own.

Help me to realize every moment that transpires is part of your perfect plan for my life. Mold me and shape me into your image, so that I can complete Your plan.

Keep me focused on your promises and guide me along the bumpy roads. Keep my heart and spirit connected with the promises you have so carefully crafted just for me.

Teach me how to grow in my faith so that You are bigger than my circumstances, and I can be a light when faced with darkness.

Let Your love fill me up with that joy that only comes from knowing You intimately. I lay all my pages at your feet believing and knowing You alone are in full control.

Allow God to be the author of your story. What is God asking you to share to encourage others?

"...For I know the plans I have for you," declares the Lord, "plans to prosper you and not to harm you, plans to give you hope and a future." ~ Jeremiah 29:11 (NIV)

"This is good, and pleases God our Savior, who wants all people to be saved and to come to a knowledge of the truth." ~ 1 Timothy 2:3-4 (NIV)

"...give thanks in all circumstances; for this is God's will for you in Christ Jesus." ~ 1 Thessalonians 5:18 (NIV)

He is My Breath

"But now, O Lord, You are our Father;
We are the clay, and You our potter; And all
we are the work of Your hand."
~ Isaiah 64:8

Has your heart ever hurt so bad you questioned God's purpose for your life? Has your heart been torn to pieces at some point by the results of a doctor's report on your health, a child or teenager's words or actions towards you, a spouse's hurtful comment? Has an unexpected loss taken your breath away?

I have been left breathless many times with many struggles; at times, feeling like I could not possibly go another day in all the madness. After the tantrum, the crying and the screaming, I found myself with the same God, face to face with the only one who consistently takes me out of the darkness.

He is still there. He is still God. He is patiently waiting to cover me with His grace and pour His love into my soul in place of the pain.

While I am in the painful places, I often miss the light, but when I look towards Him and choose Him, the joy and wisdom once again become indescribable.

PRAY

Holy Spirit, enter my heart today. Replace the pain with Your joy! Comfort me and fill me this moment with Your unconditional love so I can fulfill Your plans and be all that You have designed for me to be here on earth.

I yearn to replace my painful moments with you, Lord. Fulfill Your will and promises through my circumstances. Teach me how to release it all and breathe with You.

Help me to stop opening those doors that keep me trapped and to run with You into Your light, with You in times of darkness. Wash me white as snow, renew my soul so that I can gain the wisdom I can only get when I seek You.

Let me dwell with You as my creator, potter, and author of this story. I desire to be a manifestation of Your perfect will.

SEEK AND JOURNAL

What are you struggling with today?

Know that God has left us the Holy Spirit to comfort us and to fill us with His peace. ~Acts 4 8:31

Know that He loves you unconditionally. ~1 Chronicles 16:34

Know He is the potter of this great masterpiece which is YOU!
~Isaiah 64:8

He is My Truth

"I have told you these things, so that in me you may have peace. In this world, you will have trouble. But take heart! I have overcome the world."
~ John 16:33 (NIV)

What do I know for certain in my storms? My God has never left me and never will. I have learned this repeatedly, and when I have wanted to give up, He has shown up.

I have learned to release and lean totally on my King. When those voices in my head attempt to keep me in a state of chaos, I turn to the one who loves me. When my emotions start taking over, I know I have let go of my Savior's hands and am all in the flesh. Caught up and straight messed up, I am no longer choosing His joy.

Choosing His joy—and staying in His word—are the keys that I want to keep using to unlock those doors in my heart with Him.

Don't you?

This journey was not meant to be done alone, but hand-in-hand with Him.

PRAY

Lord, I am so grateful that You have chosen me to love, that You have given me the ability to choose You and to fight these battles with You. Father, when I get lost in my ways, and my flesh wants to win, take me to Your word and make me whole again.

The truth is that You are everlasting, never failing and always there ready to give me another chance. I am so eternally grateful for this.

My joy is greatest when I am connected to You.

I do not want to continue to fight these battles in the flesh but with Your word and in Your promises. I want to rejoice in the wisdom and knowledge that I gain for my struggles, not drown in them and give up in my circumstances.

You have chosen such a time as this to allow the great things and the trials to happen in my life. Teach me how to use it all for Your glory.

I yearn to live in Your truths and Your love and to choose Joy knowing that every day with You is a gift worth fighting for.

Thank you, Father, for not letting go even when I do.

SEEK AND JOURNAL

When the battles start taking over your emotions, fight hand in hand with God and in His word. Write down your battles today and release each one to your King.

"For we do not wrestle against flesh and blood, but against principalities, against powers, against the rulers of the darkness of this age, against spiritual hosts of wickedness in the heavenly places."
~ Ephesians 6:12

He is My Love

"Oh, give thanks to the Lord, for He is good!
For His mercy endures forever."
~ Psalm 136:1

D o you ever take a moment to think about how much God loves you? I often do, and I am sure my trials and struggles had something to do with it. It has been in those very hard places I have called on Him the most and surrendered the most to His will.

It reminds me of my kids, they are over 18 and adults, and they tend to run to me the most when they are in need. My daughter, for example, had a mega stomach ache two weeks ago and was about a forty-five minutes' drive away from home and guess who she called? Yep, Mom.

Though grateful for her call, I wish the call was to tell me how much she missed me, appreciated me, and loved me and this made me think. Oh, how much would our Lord love this from me as well? He is always there, ready to help, never failing just waiting for me to love Him.

How awesome is He? He loves me so much that He is available to me all day and gives me the choice to seek Him and worship Him; how I pray to be obedient to His call not only when I need Him.

So, today as I sit in my joyful place, I appreciate the trials that continue to show me how much He truly loves me when I seek Him and find Him.

How about you?

PRAY

So grateful to be Yours today Lord. How can I please You? How can I bring glory to Your name?

You give, give and give daily with the hope of my love and worship of You. You wait patiently and never give up on me; how I yearn today to fall at Your feet and trust You with everything You desire for me.

Abba Father I want to sit still and call on Your name and thank You for Your love and protection when I could not see it was You. Forgive me, Father, those moments when I pushed You aside and thought I had the power to accomplish things that only You could for me.

I am sorry, Father, for running ahead of You, when Your plan for my life is so perfect, and Your promises for me are so good. I am running back to You and laying it all at Your feet. I want my heart's desire to be all about You. I want to please You with my actions.

Keep me rooted in Your word and help me with my selfish ways.

SEEK AND JOURNAL

As you sit in your joyful place. Read Psalm 136 in your Bible and make a list of all of the things you are thankful for. Write to Him. He is always listening.

_____

_____

_____

_____

_____

_____

_____

_____

_____

_____

_____

_____

_____

He is My Rest

"Truly my soul waits for God; from Him comes my salvation; He is my defense; I shall not be greatly moved."
~ Psalm 62:1-2

What are you struggling with today? Have you laid it all at Jesus' feet?

So easy to ask and say, right? I know when I start to tense up around the back of my neck, and my thoughts and concerns take me to a place of unrest, I am struggling and not giving it to the one who has had me from the very beginning.

Negativity starts to creep into the things I say, and I forget who is listening and taking notes attentively to use it against me or destroy me completely. Satan himself!

I forget that the same God who brought me through and out of cancer and divorce is still the same God who is carrying me through numerous surgeries. The same God who fills me with the strength to accept and move forward with my colostomy.

Wow! and I still try to carry things on my own even after all of the battles He has fought for me and has won for me.

I had the pleasure to see Nick Vujicic, live at Calvary Chapel, Fort Lauderdale. Can I just say, amazing! He was on fire for Jesus and using his story for God's divine purpose. What I heard from God and learned from Him was, "God is not in the business of wasting my pain, my testimony, my history is God's story, not mine."

As I continue to fight this health battle, I refuse to waste God's story in me. So, I will pray, seek, journal and share because He is not only watching but expecting great things from me. I will keep pushing because my testimony belongs to Him. His plan in it is so much greater than anything I can see.

Today, know your testimony is His story, and go find someone to bless with it. God will give you strength.

He has done that for me.

PRAY

Lord, I have seen the amazing things You have done with me in my chaos and struggles. I have seen the works of Your hands in my (fill in the blank). Today, I know Your desire is for me to trust and know You. I am here Father, help me through my storms.

I want to believe everything You have for me. Help me in my moments of unbelief. Show me how to walk with You in prayer when I want to pick up the chaos and try to manage it on my own. I no longer want to keep going in circles, ending up in the same place forgetting that You are my fortress, my rock, and my salvation.

My heart's desire is to find rest and joy in You alone. Take my struggles and show me how to do this with You!

SEEK AND JOURNAL

What area of your life do you find yourself stressed? Write it down and talk to God about it. Hand it over to Him and watch Him work out miracles.

He is My Strength

"He gives power to the weak, and to those who have no might He increases strength."

~ Isaiah 40:29

actually had one full week of feeling almost normal (whatever that means) in my body. I woke up each morning and truly gave my circumstances to the only one that has control over the ups and downs of my health. I gave it to my creator who knows ALL about me!

He strengthened me from the inside out and gave me the energy I needed. It was awesome to feel good—something I do not take lightly or for granted anymore. I am so grateful that in the good days where I can forget about His miracles, I was able to see His work in me and experience Him in all that I was able to accomplish.

I know that walking and trusting Him to be in control freed me from the burden I try to carry on my own daily. I know that even when my body becomes weak, and my mind becomes foggy, I am going to continue to believe in His strength and drive in me.

So, today no matter what you are going through remember the good days and be strengthened by all that Has has done for you.

PRAY

Heavenly Father, thank you for the promises that live in Your word. I am so grateful that You do not grow weary of me and my daily requests. Thank you that You watch over me and protect and strengthen me in my weakness.

When my body and mind grow weary, I rejoice because I can draw from Your well of JOY and be renewed and restored daily.

Lord, you are so good to me. Thank you for the good days that fill me with wisdom and strength to defeat the bad days.

Renew my faith and stir my heart with Your love.

SEEK AND JOURNAL

Read Isaiah 40:28-31. What do you hear God saying to you?

He is My Light

"When Jesus spoke again to the people, he said, "I am the light of the world. Whoever follows me will never walk in darkness, but will have the light of life."
~ John 8:12 (NIV)

have a confession to make. I am not perfect. Shocked? I know. So sorry to disappoint you all. At times, I put on a face so no one can catch a glimpse of those dark parts of me. You see, I have struggled long with some things.

Now, don't you judge; this is a confession. I have struggled with being angry and silent with those I love the most. I have lived in silence many miserable days saying things and words I am sure I should not have thought about or said. In that silence, that dark box has kept me stuck. In there I could hear God's voice saying, "Desiree, you are not going to be able to fix this in your box, get out and hand it over to me,' but in true Desiree fashion and stubbornness I found myself over and over again turning from His voice and falling deeper into my darkness; sometimes falling deeper in for hours and sometimes for days. With my head going in complete circles with what I can accomplish on my own and dismissing what God can do through it all.

In those moments, I have struggled with just accepting His truth, His light, and His way. The heaviness did not allow me to pull those covers off of my eyes and see His light.

So, why am I sharing this? I want you to know that only because of Him I have been able to crawl out of that dark box. I have spent countless hours with wonderful prayer warriors God has sent my way and have prayed many days by myself for God to take over.

It is here—in my imperfections and times of darkness—I have experienced God's pure light. His truth and light have showered me with a peace I can only try to explain in these words.

Today, I might crawl out of the dark box slowly, but I crawl out. His light has allowed me to change my ways and to reflect more on what He can do through the angry moments than what I can do. I stay fixed on His word and the light that He offers me daily. I seek Him and stay close to Him in my thoughts and the crazy in my head. I no longer feel trapped where satan would love to keep me. When things start to roll out of my mouth and into my head that shouldn't be there, I move away from the dark box and into His amazing light and grace because without Him my struggle would have consumed me and those around me.

PRAY

Father, today I want to live as Your child of light. Soften me, renew me and restore me in my times of darkness. You alone know my flaws and ugly places and know the plans You have for me during these not so attractive moments.

Lord, expose anything that needs readjusting in me and bring to light what is keeping me in the dark. Thank you for choosing me to see You in your greatness. Continue to remove me from those moments that fog my vision and draw me away from seeing You and Your plans for me. Replace my stubbornness with Your love and grant me Your peace so that I can be more and more like You.

Father, teach me how to focus on Your strength, not mine, Your control not mine. Remind me that I cannot direct my next breath so how can I control anything else. You are the place I should run to each time, help me, Lord, to do this each and every moment of my day. You alone Father allow me life. I want to spend this week seeing You through all of my circumstances. Giving You everything I cannot change.

Thank you, Lord, for being my light and shining Your love on me over and over again!

SEEK AND JOURNAL

Believe in God's light and give Him all of your storms. Write them all down and pray, pray, pray.

"Let your light so shine before men, that they may see your good works, and glorify your Father in heaven." ~ Matthew 5:16

"For God so loved the world that He gave His only begotten Son, that whoever believes in Him shall not perish but have everlasting life. ~ John 3:16

He is My Anchor

"We have this hope as an anchor for the soul, firm and secure. It enters the inner sanctuary behind the curtain, where our forerunner, Jesus, has entered on our behalf. He has become a high priest forever..."
~ Hebrews 6:19-20 (NIV)

Life is such a fantastic storm... complex, wonderful, and confusing all at the same time. How we respond to each storm usually depends on where we place our hope and where we set our feet down. I often talk about being focused on our flesh, the world or being focused on our Jesus.

Where are you today? Are your hopes in Him or are you drifting?

Are you anchored in Him?

When I find myself drifting and drowning in my storms, I know that my hope is not set on the one who is constant, never-changing, the "El Olam." (Genesis 14:19)

Somehow in trying to do life I have shifted my focus and find myself losing control of what is important. Life does not seem so bright, and the joy that fills my heart when I am grounded starts to slowly drift away.

I like to visualize this as a ship—one of those huge ones. Imagine what would happen if they did not anchor the ships correctly? Well, it's no different than our hope and faith during the storms.

Pay close attention, if the ship is not anchored correctly and if your trust and hope are not always on our King you will drown. You will be lost at sea when the storms hit. You might even sink.

Can you relate?

When I start to place my hope in this world or the circumstances, it becomes so difficult to find joy and peace. I am caught out there somewhere in the abyss, holding on to the wrong things and placing my hope on things of this world, which from experience never fully satisfies.

Today, let's anchor ourselves firmly in Him. When the storms come into our lives, let's put our hope in the one who has never left us and who keeps all of His promises... no matter what.

PRAY

Lord, I want my faith and hope in You to be unshakeable! Keep my eyes, mind, and spirit fixed on You. Keep me grounded in You, not my storms. I desire for my life to align only with Your word. Teach me, heavenly Father, how to anchor myself in You! My heart's desire is to be close to You and to seek You in my storms. Draw me close when I start to drift, when the storms come in fierce and strong, and I find myself sinking.

Holy Spirit, transform my hope and faith into one that is unmovable. Help me to run every time to Your word and ground myself in your promises that will fill me with the joy and peace only knowing You can give.

Lord, those days when it gets so hard to move on, restore my soul and restore my faith back to You. I am so grateful that I can anchor myself in only You. When I drift, help me to place my faith and hope in all that You have planned for my life. Help me to believe and be grateful for all that You have brought me through thus far.

Thank you that my hope does not have to be on the things of this world but in Christ, Your Son.

Today, Lord I stand firmly anchored in You.

SEEK AND JOURNAL

Anchor yourself in your King. When you find yourself drifting or even sinking remember, He is your hope.

"May the God of hope fill you with all joy and peace as you trust in Him, so that you may overflow with hope by the power of the Holy Spirit." ~ Romans 15:13 (NIV)

"Praise be to the God and Father of our Lord Jesus Christ! In His great mercy, He has given us new birth into a living hope through the resurrection of Jesus Christ from the dead," ~ 1 Peter 1:3 (NIV)

He is My Place

"He may let them rest in a feeling of security,
but His eyes are on their ways."
~ Job 24:23 (NIV)

Every time my tank is depleted, I go to my place with Him. Do you have a place? A place where you can see Him, and you know for sure He can see you? A place where His peace and love pour into your soul like hot chocolate on a cold breezy day?

He is there, and He has designed that place just so you can see His beauty and His love for you. I often wonder when I am there what does He see? Does He see what I feel? Does He see my pain, my struggles, my constant battles with things? Does He see the beauty in me?

The beauty of this place reminds me that I am His and replenishes my soul with His joy.

PRAY

Father, mornings like today, when I wake up right where I started emotionally yesterday, I know I need to meet You in Your word and in the place You designed just for me. My body is tired today, and my mind is troubled and confused with some things.

Will you please take them from me?

I am in that spot again Lord, where You constantly have to pull me out of. I have lost my peace and know I need to run to You to find it again. I lift my body and mind to You, Father, once again and yearn for Your Joy in my life. I refuse to give up even if I have to ask You every day to help me out. I want to dwell with You today and rejoice in the beauty that You so generously have given me for free.

Take me through this week, hand in hand, and comfort me with Your presence. Teach me how to keep working on fixing my eyes on only You and believing that Your will is perfect. You know where I am right now, and I trust that You will show me the way and bring me back to that perfect place of Joy in You.

SEEK AND JOURNAL

Go to your joyful place and connect with Him today.

He is My Feet

"Teach me your way, Lord, that I may rely on Your faithfulness; give me an undivided heart, that I may fear Your name."
~ Psalm 86:11 (NIV)

Have you ever found yourself going in the wrong direction? The one God was clearly telling you not to go in? Did it turn out well for you? If you are like me, not so much.

What I know is that each time I take that turn, I come out more depleted and deceived than the first time, with a gaping hole where God is yearning and calling to get in. In every wrong turn (emotional, financial, spiritual, physical) He is there knocking and waiting, ready to fill that void I so eagerly am trying to fill on my own.

See, in those moments, I forget of His amazing love. I forget that His way is the right way. I forget that when I choose Him, the path is clearer, not perfect but so much better. (John 14:6)

When I choose to walk with Him, the spaces in my heart start to fill with His Joy and peace, not consumed by my pains and my emotions. Oh! how grateful I am for His patience with me as I fail each and every time in my turns.

During this His season will you choose to grab His hand. Walk with Him and know Him in your turns. I know I sure do!

I can't walk a day without Him!

PRAY

Lord, I want to walk side by side with You. I want to ask You so much that I don't get right now. Please redirect my wrong turns. Show me Your face, when my decisions do not reflect or align with Your plan.

Dear Father, as I walk today, hold my hand tightly and embrace me when I am not living Your designed purpose for my life. I want to come to You as a child and be held in Your loving embrace while I walk in the chaos of my days.

Thank you, Lord, that You have created a space in my heart where You alone fit perfectly. Help me to fill it with those things You have so many times shown me when I am headed in the wrong direction. Teach me how to replace the selfishness with selflessness, the anger with Your love, and disappointments with Your promises.

Lord, I choose to walk with You and to be filled with the joy and hope that You alone can fill. When the day gets hectic, lead me to Your warm embrace and help me to be complete with only You!

SEEK AND JOURNAL

Are you walking with God? Write down all of the different areas you are choosing to walk with God.

Desiree Montalvo-Holt

He is My Path

"He says, "Be still, and know that I am God;
I will be exalted among the nations, I will
be exalted in the earth!"
~ Psalm 46:10 (NIV)

Do I go this way? Do I say this or not say that? When I start my morning with these questions, I am likely to be headed in the wrong direction and surely not to find the path and peace God has designed specifically for me in my day. So, what is my go-to, to find God's joy and peace each morning?

Here you go...

First, I start by praying with Him one on one. If I allow distractions to take over, I have epic fails in this area and trust me the distractions will come as soon as you start, so beware and stay strong.

Second, I go to His word, seeking His path for me in the words I read. I choose a book from the bible, a devotion from my many books, a specific bible verse, a Christian blog post and start seeking. Whatever leads you right to Him and connects you to Him.

Third, after seeking Him in His word, I journal and engage in conversation with Him. I write, write and write. God will lead. Trust me; He has for me.

The days when I start this way-my heart and walk aligned with Him-I begin to let go, reflect, repent and feel the peace and JOY He had for me all along.

Today, will you join me in praying, seeking, and journaling so that our walk is more a reflection of the life our King desires for you and me!

PRAY

Holy Spirit, lead me on this walk with You! Take over my mind and my heart when distractions clutter my time with You, Lord. I want to be complete with You Father, hold me tightly and keep me close. Take all that is not of You away and fill me with Your grace and mercies. Wash me clean and continue to mold me into who You created me to be.

Help me this morning to focus on Your love and seek Your ways. To fix my eyes on the amazing things You surround me with. My heart's desire is to only trust in You and Your word. Help me to see Your will in my walk and to stay on the path You have designed for me to follow.

When my pace becomes hurried, slow me down, remind me You are in control of my every step. Tap me on the shoulder and fill me with Your wisdom.

Help me to be still enough to not only hear You but strong enough to do all of the things You have designed for me to do.

SEEK AND JOURNAL

Be still today and know that He is God. Read Psalm 46. Pray, seek and journal with Him.

He is My Life-Line

"Trust in the Lord with all your heart and lean not on your own understanding; in all your ways submit to Him, and He will make your paths straight."
~Proverbs 3:5-6 (NIV)

When I think of every time I have been in the hospital, attached to all types of machines and have been poked by evil needles. I sit back and rejoice, knowing God allowed the surgeries and allowed everything for a higher purpose. I am still alive because of Him. It is because of His grace and mercy I am here. He alone has given me the strength to keep on pushing. I can celebrate another day of life and be grateful for all the storms that I have won holding on to Him.

He has allowed me to survive twelve surgeries, Hodgkin's disease, and so many things that I could not even see. He loves me so much that He saw all of this before it happened and equipped me with all that I would need to survive it emotionally and physically.

Today, I am a better version of me because of Him, and though I still need a lot of molding, I love that He loves me so much to help me see a glimpse of heaven in each miracle He has manifested in me.

I am not sure what you are going through; but know that if you do this with Him, you will come out victorious. You will be full of everything He desires in you, and in return, you will experience His joy!

PRAY

Heavenly Father, Holy-Spirit I want to draw from You today. I want to open up my heart to Your love and trust fully in You. I have seen the miracles in my daily circumstances. I have seen You calm the storms that have tried to destroy me, and I have seen the blessings from the pain when I fully put my trust in You.

Continue to guide and teach me how to walk with You and drink from, Your well of peace. I desire today to seek You and know you regardless of the things that surround me and try to steal my joy.

I give You all I am struggling with today knowing where I have been and how you have pulled me through. I trust you, Father, because I know you love me!

SEEK AND JOURNAL

Seek God in Psalm 136. Make Him your life-line.

He is My Rock

"There is no fear in love. But perfect love drives out fear because fear has to do with punishment. The one who fears is not made perfect in love. We love because He first loved us."
~ 1 John 4:18-19 (NIV)

D o you find it challenging to sit still and remove all of the chaos going on in your head? I do too! At times I sit ready to be all in. I mean all in, in His presence, and it starts well but in seconds there goes my head everywhere else (bills, laundry, pains and aches, text messages, and of course social media) and it all starts to draw me from His spirit. Is this how you feel? Overwhelmed? Isn't it such a struggle? Want to know what God has taught me?

To worship, worship, worship! I start my day in worship, and it leads me into His presence, away from the worldly ordeals. As soon I decide to worship, I am led into His word and totally consumed by His love for me. His covering is around me, and I am one with Him (again, don't let me fool you, many times I fall and have to come back up to worship again) Sometimes, just sitting down and listening to worship still does not work, so I play another song and try again. Thank God for His second chances.

So, today will you turn on your favorite worship song and seek His love with me in prayer and worship!

PRAY

I want to be in love with You, my Lord. Help me to discover what works for me to get closer and closer to You. Shake me from my ways. Move me when You need me to see You and hear You. Take hold of the thoughts that consume me and do not allow me to close Your spirit out.

Teach me how to adore and worship You. I want to fully rejoice in all that You have in store for me. "Rejoice in the Lord always: and again I say, Rejoice!" ~ *Philippians 4:4 (NIV)*

When I open my eyes each morning, I want my heart to rejoice in You. Guide me today. Father, You know exactly what I need today and what I need to get rid of. Remove my fleshy desires that hinder my walk with You. Remove all that draws me further and further from Your love.

Lord, in my flesh, I am always trying to fulfill my personal desires and trying to take control. Take me from my mess and flesh and fill me with Your loving spirit.

Today, I let go of all of the things that cause me worry, fears, and troubles and allow Your love to fill me with Your peace. Consume me with Your unconditional love. Fill the empty places in my soul.

Lord, I come to You today in worship and pray to receive all of the love and grace You have prepared for me. Teach me how to rejoice in Your word and carry me into Your loving presence.

SEEK AND JOURNAL

Listen to your favorite worship song. Meet God in worship and journal with Him.

He is My Friend

"Dear friends, let us love one another, for love comes from God. Everyone who loves has been born of God and knows God."
~ 1 John 4:7 (NIV)

wonder how the world would be if we loved like our Lord? Selfless and unconditional. That awesome AGAPE LOVE! I know I struggle daily with this type of love. Does your love look like this? Or, does God—and the people you call friends and family—have to do something for you to choose to love them? OUCH! Deep, right?

I know if God asked me that question every day, I would have to check myself, and I would be guilty of selfish and conditional love. So, how do I then love like You Lord? How do I not live in my shell of non-love because I did not get my way?

It made me think, what if God put such conditions on His love for me. I would be in so much trouble every moment of the day. So, today I got a wakeup call (again), and I choose to pray for God to submerge me in His type of love and teach me to be more like Him.

PRAY

Lord, as I sit here contemplating on Your love, lead me to Your arms where I can find Your Agape love. When I feel lonely, unloved, and afraid seeking love in this world, lead me to the love that You so freely offer me. Forgive me when I reject You Father and push You away. Draw me close when I want to run away.

Thank you that even in my tantrums You stand there just watching in love as I call my life circumstances unfair. You stand there patiently offering Your love and comfort in Your word. Help me Father during these blurry moments when I am being selfish. Help me to run to Your love.

Lord, teach me how to embrace Your love because I so desire to love as You love me, Father. I am so grateful that Your love is not based on what I do or even who I am. Thank you that I do not have to depend on this world to complete me with this love.

Help me today to not only seek Your love but also help me to accept and live fulfilled in Your love. Show me how to love others your way. I know I fail each and every time Father, but I desire to be more and more like You today.

Humble me today to walk in Your agape love, to speak in Your agape love and to live in Your agape love. I stand here Lord in your presence, excited that my Joy and love today and every day comes from only knowing You. Today, I give You my heart so You can mold me and replace the conditions and selfishness in my heart with You.

Lord, I want Your greatness and love to show in me.

SEEK AND JOURNAL

Read 1 John 4:9-11 and Proverbs 8:17. What are you hearing God saying to you?

_____

_____

_____

_____

_____

_____

_____

_____

_____

_____

_____

_____

He is My Thoughts

"Look at the birds of the air, they do not sow or store away in barns, and yet your heavenly Father feeds them. Are you not much more valuable than they?"

~ Matthew 6:26 (NIV)

Do you find yourself thinking in your sleep? Thinking while you drive? Thinking while you are sitting at the bus stop waiting for your children? Your questions and thoughts might go something like this: What am I going to wear? What am I going to cook or eat? How am I going to accomplish all this holiday shopping and keep everyone happy?

Yes, it is endless and most of the time it all takes care of itself, or not. Why? Because at the end of the day we can find peace knowing God is in full control, not us. He has already provided. His will shall be done in your life if you just let Him in and believe.

I truly have learned this the hard way. So, today when your thoughts and the events of our world are consuming you, visualize yourself placing it all at Gods feet. Remember you need Him through the crazy moments. He is the only one who can. He created you! He created everything that surrounds you.

So, as the world continues to unravel, breathe... and give your thoughts to the One who has overcome the world (John 16:33).

PRAY

Lord, comfort me from the chaos of my thoughts. As chaos begins to consume my joy and peace through my day, teach me how to lay it all at Your feet. Help me to trust that You have the solutions to the unanswered questions and moments in my life.

Lord, replace any confusion with the truth of Your promises in Your word. I no longer want to pretend like I have it all together. I fully know I don't, *without You.* There might be moments of personal success which fool me of such control, but in the end, it is only through You I can accomplish all I set out to do during my day.

When my schedule becomes overwhelming, show me the accomplishments that matter most to You. Show me how to fill my day with You and Your love. Remind me that You alone know the plans You have for me.

Lord, I don't always do the right thing, have the right thoughts or pray the right prayer, so please take over and fill me with You.

Move me through this day filled with You and allow me to be a blessing to all who come around me. Don't let me get stuck in the moments of my chaos.

Help me to rejoice in Your total sovereignty over my life. Still me, so that my steps align with yours. Let my thoughts be Your thoughts today.

SEEK AND JOURNAL

What can you hand over to God today? Lord, I give You...

He is My Fortress

> **"I am the Alpha and the Omega,"**
> **says the Lord God, "who is, and who was,**
> **and who is to come, the Almighty."**
> ~ Revelation 1:8 (NIV)

am stuck... *again?*

Do you feel this way sometimes? Stuck in your ways, or stuck in vicious patterns that draw you further and further from acting how God would want you to act? If you do, trust me, you are not the only one.

I find myself turning to everyone around me for answers and turning to my own thoughts (not the best place to be sometimes) to try and come out of that dark place, only to find myself a few days later—or a month later—back where I started (angry, mad, disappointed, etc.) and asking, "Why me?" again.

I work so hard to get out of my thoughts and dwell in God's presence and will, but the cycle keeps sucking me in, and I get lost in my thoughts and forget who God really is!

When I pray, He takes hold of me and reminds me that:

He is the Almighty One (Rev 1:8).

He is the Alpha and Omega (Rev 22:13).

He is the Light of the world (John 8:12).

He is the One who sets us free (John 8:36).

He is Peace (Eph.2:14)

He is The Way (John 1:1), and I am reminded that
in His presence, my thoughts become lighter and
I fall easier at His feet.

Will you give Him your thoughts today in exchange for His Way,
Light, Freedom, and Peace?

PRAY

Lord, feed my soul. Fill my spirit. Lead me to the spiritual tools
that keep me in Your word. Please take over; I surrender to Your
ultimate will for my life. When my thoughts push me one way,
and I find myself back in that dark place of disappointment, pain,
and anger, draw me out into Your light.

Rid me of myself, take me from the chaos that never seems to end
and leaves me void and empty in my heart, seeking those things
Lord that You have not designed for me.

I long for Your peace and love. Today, I want to exchange my thoughts for Your joy. My darkness for Your light. I pray Lord You lift the walls that keep caving in on me and teach me how to live freely in Your word. May my actions continue to be renewed and refreshed by seeking You more deeply in my day.

Lord, I want to stop asking, "Why me?" and trust You know the Why and the path I need. Thank you for never leaving me.

Father, help me to step out of me and mirror more of You.

I come before You Lord and pour out all of my feelings of inadequacy, weaknesses, and inferiority and replace them with all of the truths You have promised in Your mighty word.

Lord, restore my thoughts and soul. I do not want to be stuck in my ways anymore that keep me stagnant in my darkness. Unchain me from my thoughts so that I can be free in You.

Father, reveal Yourself in me and be the vine that supports and gives me strength and courage to keep going each day.

SEEK AND JOURNAL

Release all of those things that keep you stuck.

_____

_____

_____

SEEK AND JOURNAL

Use the pages that follow as you need...

Desiree Montalvo-Holt

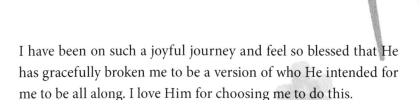

I have been on such a joyful journey and feel so blessed that He has gracefully broken me to be a version of who He intended for me to be all along. I love Him for choosing me to do this.

With every book purchased, a percentage of the proceeds will go toward obtaining materials needed to create and deliver "JOY bags" to those who are battling a storm.

Together we can Make Joy Contagious!

I'd also like to personally invite you to visit:
instagram.com/makingjoycontagious

In His Joy,

Desiree